easy origami

EASY ANIMAL
Origami

by Christopher L. Harbo

Ⓡ **www.raintreepublishers.co.uk**
Visit our website to find out
more information about
Raintree books.

To order:
☎ Phone 0845 6044371
🖨 Fax +44 (0) 1865 312263
💻 Email myorders@raintreepublishers.co.uk

Customers from outside the UK please telephone +44 1865 312262

Raintree is an imprint of Capstone Global Library Limited, a company incorporated in
England and Wales having its registered office at 7 Pilgrim Street, London, EC4V 6LB –
Registered company number: 6695582

First published by Capstone Press in 2011
First published in the United Kingdom in 2012

The m_____ated.

Printed and bound in China by Leo Paper Products Ltd

ISBN 978 1 406 24264 5
16 15 14 13 12
10 9 8 7 6 5 4 3 2 1

British Library Cataloguing in Publication Data
A full catalogue record for this book is available from the British Library.

Disclaimer
All the Internet addresses (URLs) given in this book were valid at the time of going to
press. However, due to the dynamic nature of the Internet, some addresses may have
changed, or sites may have changed or ceased to exist since publication. While the
publisher regrets any inconvenience this may cause readers, no responsibility for any
such changes can be accepted by the publisher.

ABOUT THE AUTHOR

Christopher L. Harbo loves origami. He began folding
paper several years ago and hasn't stopped.
In addition to decorative origami, he also enjoys
folding paper aeroplanes. When he's not making
origami, Christopher spends his free time reading
Japanese comic books and watching films.

TABLE OF CONTENTS

PAPER ZOO

Welcome to the origami zoo! As zookeeper, you'll turn paper squares into amazing animals. Tucked inside this book are seven of the easiest origami animals ever created. You'll fold a dog's head, a fluttering butterfly, a beautiful swan, and much more. Jump in and start folding your paper zoo!

MATERIALS

Origami is a simple art that doesn't use many materials. You'll only need the following things to complete the projects in this book:

Origami paper: Square origami paper comes in many fun colours and sizes. You can use 15 by 15 centimetres square paper for the models in this book, unless the instructions tell you to use a different paper size. You can buy this paper in most craft shops.

A4-sized paper: Not all origami models begin with a square. Use A4 paper (210 by 297 millimetres) when needed.

Ruler: Some models use measurements to complete. A ruler will help you measure.

Pencil: Use a pencil when you need to mark spots you measure with the ruler.

Craft supplies: Pens and other craft supplies will help you to decorate your models.

FOLDING TECHNIQUES

Folding paper is easier when you understand basic origami folds and symbols. Practise the folds on this list before trying the models in this book. Turn back to this list if you get stuck on a tricky step, or ask an adult for help.

Valley Folds are represented by a dashed line. One side of the paper is folded against the other like a book. A sharp fold is made by running your finger along the fold line.

Mountain Folds are represented by a pink or white dashed and dotted line. The paper is folded sharply behind the model.

Squash Folds are formed by lifting one edge of a pocket. The pocket gets folded again so the spine gets flattened. The existing fold lines become new edges.

Inside reverse folds are made by opening a pocket slightly. Then you fold the model inside itself along existing fold lines.

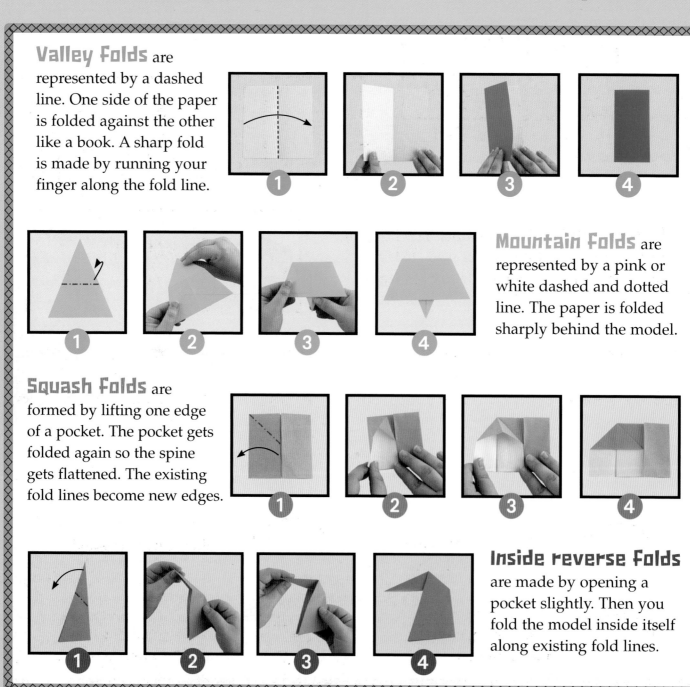

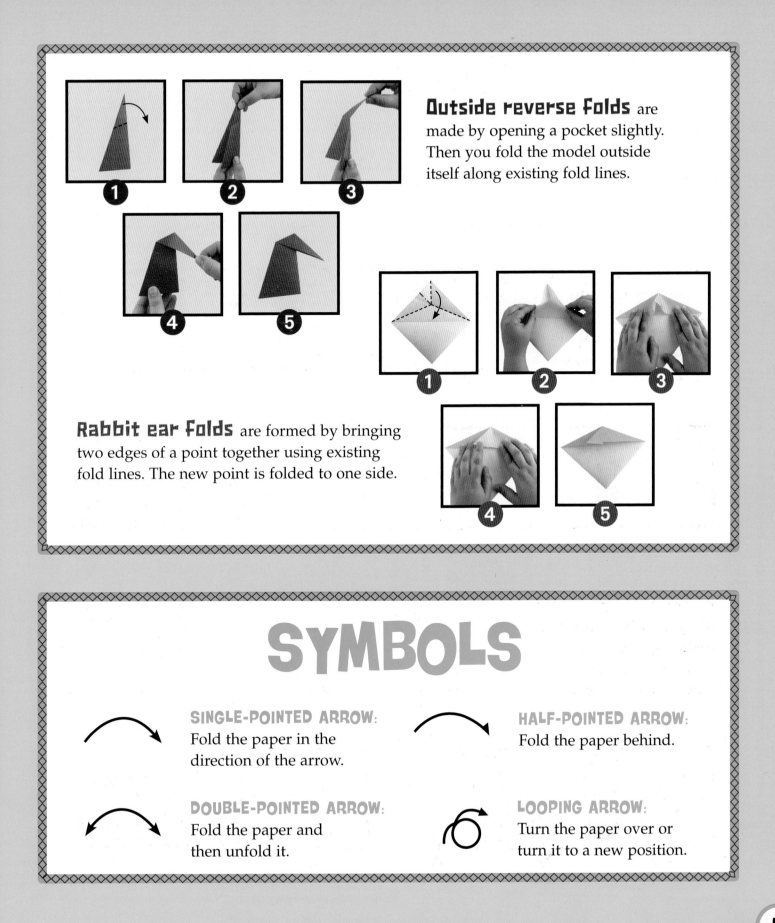

Outside reverse Folds are made by opening a pocket slightly. Then you fold the model outside itself along existing fold lines.

Rabbit ear Folds are formed by bringing two edges of a point together using existing fold lines. The new point is folded to one side.

SYMBOLS

SINGLE-POINTED ARROW:
Fold the paper in the direction of the arrow.

HALF-POINTED ARROW:
Fold the paper behind.

DOUBLE-POINTED ARROW:
Fold the paper and then unfold it.

LOOPING ARROW:
Turn the paper over or turn it to a new position.

FLOPPY-EARED dog

Traditional model

Folding this paper dog is easy!
In just five simple steps you'll
have a floppy-eared pup.

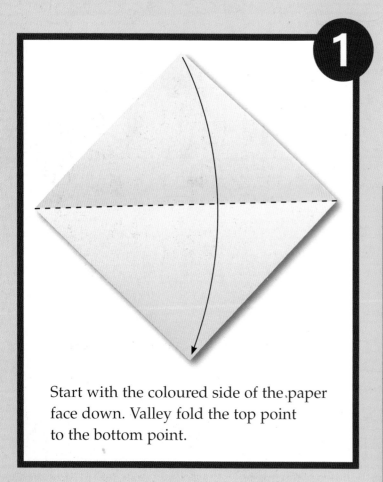

1

Start with the coloured side of the paper
face down. Valley fold the top point
to the bottom point.

2

Valley fold the left point to
the right point and unfold.

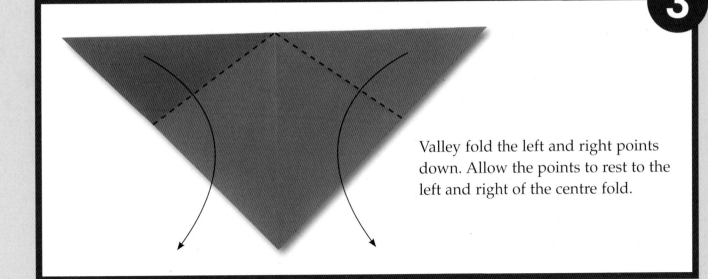

3

Valley fold the left and right points down. Allow the points to rest to the left and right of the centre fold.

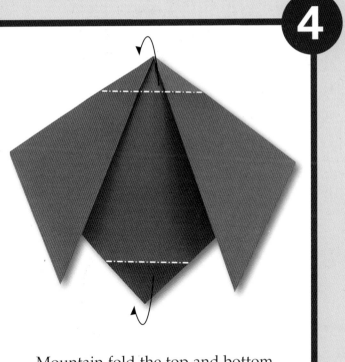

4

Mountain fold the top and bottom points behind the model.

5

Now give your pup a friendly face!

PURR-FECT cat

Traditional model

Some cats have tall, pointy ears. This cat copies those fancy features purr-fectly.

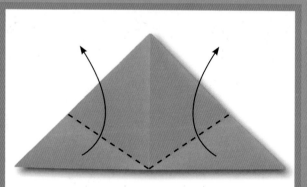

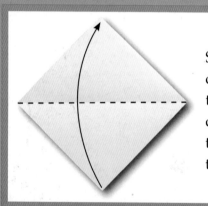

1

Start with the coloured side of the paper face down. Valley fold the bottom point to the top point.

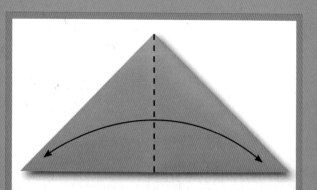

Valley fold the left point to the right point and unfold.

2

Valley fold the left and right points up. Allow the points to rest to the left and right of the centre fold.

3

4

Valley fold the top point about halfway down the centre fold.

5

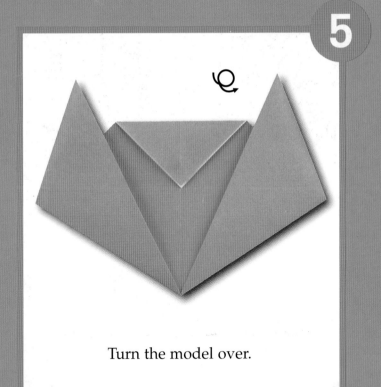

Turn the model over.

6

Add large eyes and a small nose to bring your cat to life.

SECRET tip Don't forget to add whiskers to your cat. Try using string, wool, or straws.

11

FLAPPING butterfly

Traditional model

Butterflies float through the air from flower to flower. This butterfly will amaze you with its graceful fluttering.

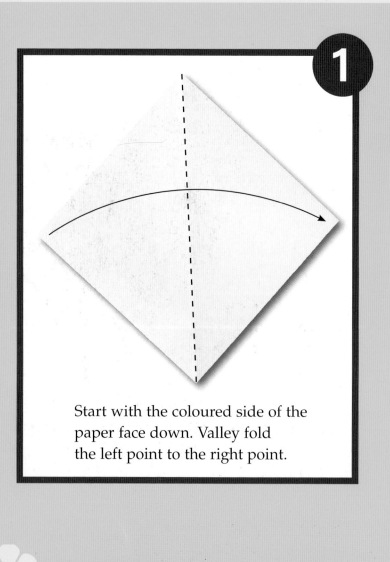

1

Start with the coloured side of the paper face down. Valley fold the left point to the right point.

2

Valley fold the top point to the bottom point.

3

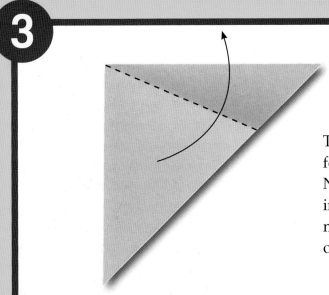

Take the top layer and valley fold the bottom point up. Note how the fold begins in the top-left corner of the model. Repeat this valley fold on the back side of the model.

4

Unfold the top wing halfway. Repeat this step on the back wing.

Your butterfly is ready to fly. Press on its back to make the wings flutter.

5

SECRET tip

Curl the tips of your butterfly's wings up slightly with a pencil. Your butterfly is now an ocean stingray!

CROUCHING bunny

Traditional model

Rabbits crouch down in the grass when they eat. This folded bunny looks ready to nibble the top off a carrot.

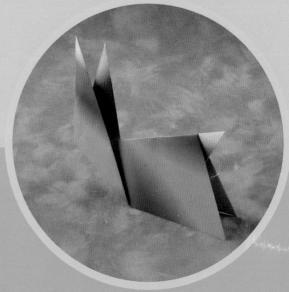

1 Start with the coloured side of the paper face down. Valley fold the top point to bottom point and unfold.

2 Valley fold the top-left edge to the centre fold. Valley fold the bottom-left edge to the centre fold.

3 Valley fold the right point along the edge from step 2.

14

4

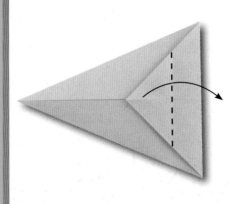

Valley fold the point across the right edge of the model. The fold should be made about 2·5 cm from the right edge.

5

Valley fold the top-right point to the bottom-right point.

6

At the left point, use scissors to make a 7·6 cm cut. The cut should go along the model's back.

7

Valley fold the top flap up. This fold starts where the cut from step 6 ends. Repeat this valley fold on the back side of the model.

Help your bunny hop to the nearest carrot patch!

8

SECRET tip In step 7, fold the ears at slightly different angles. Doing this will help you to see both ears when the model is completed.

SPOTTED ladybird

Traditional model

Did you know ladybirds come in different colours? Use red paper to make the popular ladybird. Or use purple paper to make a ladybird that's a bit different.

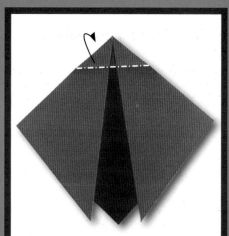

1

Start with the coloured side of the paper face down. Valley fold the top point to the bottom point.

2

Valley fold the left point to the right point and unfold.

3

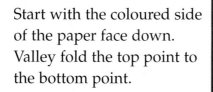

Valley fold the left and right points down. Allow the points to rest to the left and right of the centre fold.

4

Mountain fold the top point behind the model.

5

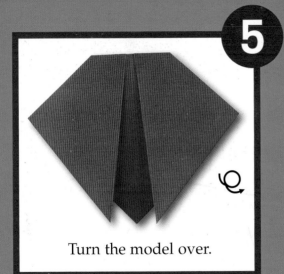

Turn the model over.

6

Valley fold the upside-down triangle at the top of the model. This fold is made about 0·64 cm below the top edge. A smaller triangle will now stick out at the top.

7

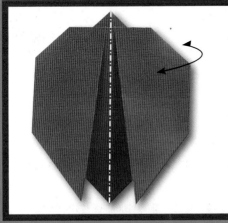

Turn the model over.

8

Mountain fold the left and right points behind the model.

9

Mountain fold the right side of the model behind the left side and unfold.

10

Your ladybird is ready for spots. Draw them on with a black pen.

SECRET
tip
Curl the wings of your ladybird upwards slightly to make the model look more lifelike.

PERCHED parrot

Traditional model

Are you looking for a paper pet that won't make a peep? This folded parrot will keep you company without ever saying a word.

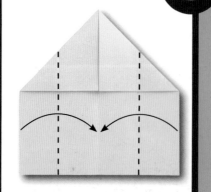

1

Start with the coloured side of the paper face down. Valley fold the left edge to the right edge and unfold.

2

Valley fold the top-left corner to the centre fold. Valley fold the top-right corner to the centre fold.

3

Valley fold the left side to the centre fold. Valley fold the right side to the centre fold.

4

Mountain fold the right side of the model behind the left side.

5

Valley fold the bottom-right corner up and to the left. This fold begins on the right side of the model where another fold ends. After making a sharp fold, unfold the corner.

6

Inside reverse fold on the folds from step 5. This fold allows the bottom-right edge to swing up inside the model. When finished, a small square sticks out from the left side of the model.

7

Valley fold the top-left corner of the small square to the bottom-right corner.

10

Inside reverse fold on the folds from step 9. This fold allows the point to stick out the left side of the model. Then turn the model slightly to the left.

8

Inside reverse fold on the folds from step 7. This fold allows the top-left corner to tuck inside the square.

9

Valley fold the top point to the left and unfold.

11

Your parrot looks ready to sit on your finger.

SWIMMING SWAN

Traditional model

Cranes, ducks, and other birds are popular origami models. This model uses both sides of the paper to form the royal swan.

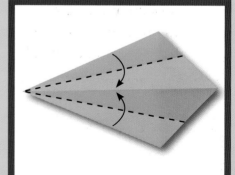

1

Start with the coloured side of the paper face down. Valley fold the top point to the bottom point and unfold.

2

Valley fold the top-right edge to the centre fold. Valley fold the bottom-right edge to the centre fold.

3

Turn the model over.

4

Valley fold the top-left edge to the centre fold. Valley fold the bottom-left edge to the centre fold.

5

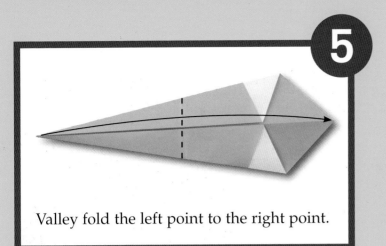

Valley fold the left point to the right point.

6

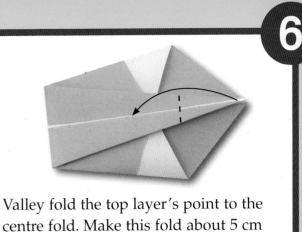

Valley fold the top layer's point to the centre fold. Make this fold about 5 cm to the left of the point.

7

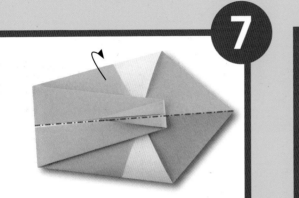

Mountain fold the top half of the model behind the bottom half.

8

Pull the swan's beak up and to the right. The beak should point up and to the left. Press the swan's beak firmly to hold the folds in place.

9

Pull the swan's neck up and to the left. When standing, the neck should point slightly to the right. Press the base of the neck to hold the folds in place.

10

Imagine your royal swan floating across a pond.

SECRET tip Line up three small swans behind one large swan. They will look like three cygnets following their mother.

READ more

My First Origami Book: Things That Go, Nick Robinson (Dover Publications, 2012)

Origami for Children, Mari Ono and Roshin Ono (Cico, 2008)

Origami Ooh La La!: Origami for Performance and Play, Jeremy Shafer (Createspace, 2010)

Origami Zoo: An Amazing Collection of Folded Paper Animals, Robert J. Lang (St. Martin's Griffin, 2006)

INTERNET sites

You can find other interesting origami models on the websites below, along with step-by-step guides on how to make each model.

www.activityvillage.co.uk/origami_for_kids.htm

www.enchantedlearning.com/crafts/origami/